IMAGES
of Scotland

KIRKLISTON

IMAGES
of Scotland

KIRKLISTON

Compiled by
Kirkliston Local History Archive

TEMPUS

First published 1998
Copyright © Kirkliston Local History Archive, 1998

Tempus Publishing Limited
The Mill, Brimscombe Port,
Stroud, Gloucestershire, GL5 2QG

ISBN 0 7524 1131 4

Typesetting and origination by
Tempus Publishing Limited
Printed in Great Britain by
Midway Clark Printing, Wiltshire

Contents

Introduction   7

1.   The Village   9

2.   The Land   45

3.   Industry and Commerce   57

4.   Education   75

5.   Recreation and Leisure   85

6.   Events   99

7.   People   115

Acknowledgments   128

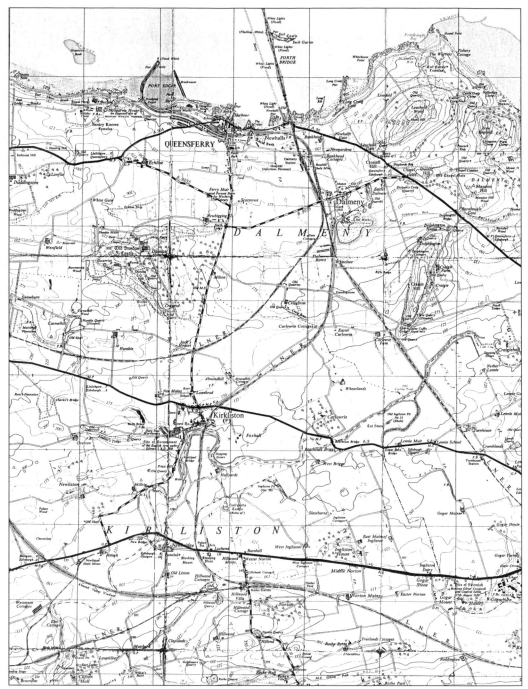

Map from 1947 showing Kirkliston in relation to the surrounding countryside. The A9 road from Edinburgh to Stirling runs east-west through the village, with the A8 Edinburgh-Glasgow road and the Edinburgh-Glasgow railway to the south. The Edinburgh-Aberdeen line crosses the Forth Bridge and the branch line from Ratho Station to Dalmeny runs through the village.

Aerial view of Kirkliston in 1952. The distillery is prominent in the foreground; the ploughed field, now filled with housing, is Gateside Farm. The foundations of the Manse Road council housing development can be seen on the left. The Glebe, in the centre, was then undeveloped, as were the two empty fields at the top of the picture on Newmains and Almondhill farmlands.

Introduction

A settlement has existed at Kirkliston since at least the twelfth century when it was simply known as Liston. The prefix Kirk was added in the fourteenth century. Of the buildings from that time only the Norman door of the parish church remains - it dates from around 1200.

The development of the village, standing as it does on the old road from Edinburgh to Stirling close to the Union Canal from Edinburgh to Falkirk, a mile north of the main Edinburgh to Glasgow road, two miles south of the Forth rail and road bridges and adjacent to Edinburgh Airport, has been much influenced by the transport systems associated with it. The great civil engineering projects attracted many workers, some of whom stayed on after construction was completed.

In June 1298, King Edward I camped with his army at Kirkliston on his way to meet the forces of William Wallace at the Battle of Falkirk. In 1663, King Charles I travelled by on his way to Linlithgow. In 1745, 'Bonnie Prince Charlie' passed through the village with his followers on his abortive march from Glenfinnan to Derby. Robert Burns, at the commencement of his highland tour with William Nicol, passed the night of 24 August 1787 at Castle House, then an inn. Queen Victoria, on her first visit to Scotland in 1842, was met near Linlithgow by the Duke of Buccleuch who escorted her to his palace at Dalkeith. On the way the last change of horses took place at Kirkliston.

Prior to the Industrial Revolution and the arrival of manufacturing, the village and the parish were entirely dependent on the land and our predecessors lived in an essentially rural economy. What industry there was functioned in support of farming, such as farriers, masons, wheelwrights and other tradesmen. The only exception was the distillery, which as far as we know, was established at the end of the eighteenth century. With the upsurge of development in the Victorian era came improved communications, in all senses of the word and with it came the camera as a simple means of pictorial record. This book is a partial account of the last hundred years and it is hoped by the authors that it will bring back memories of past times to all who have been connected with the area over the years including servicemen stationed at RAF Turnhouse and construction workers from the great bridge and motorway programmes of the 1960s. It is hoped it will also appeal to those who have moved to other parts of the United Kingdom, emigrants and their descendants and, of course, to the many who have spent their entire lives here or who have now chosen Kirkliston as a place to live.

One

The Village

Aerial view of High Street, Path Brae and Newliston Road. This picture from the 1930s clearly shows the 'backlands' between Station Road and the church, where much grazing of livestock took place. The white rectangle in the bottom right hand corner is the base of the maypole in the swing park in Station Road. The church hall (formerly the Free Church) is right centre, opposite Castle House in the High Street. Finnie's market garden which lies from the top corner of The Square along behind the church hall is now entirely occupied by houses. The railway with its level crossing gates and distillery siding is clearly visible.

STREET, KIRKLISTON

Main Street, Kirkliston, when telegraph poles were visible. On the left can be seen one of Kirkliston's earliest lamp standards. It was erected, probably, in the early 1880's from funds raised at a lecture by Peter McLagan of Pumpherston, MP for Linlithgow, who lived for a time at Cliftonhall with the Bell family.

Boathouse Bridge on the old Edinburgh-Stirling road was built in the latter part of the eighteenth century. A map of 1748 showed a ferry boat crossing the river, and another dated 1794 showed the bridge below an ancient ford uncrossable when the river was in spate. Frequent flooding caused concern and an additional arch was added to the north end of the bridge in 1834 by the Trustees of the Turnpike Road. The engineers were Robert Stevenson and Son, Edinburgh, and the stone came from Humbie Quarry. The bridge was widened in 1950 and the photograph shows the heightened supports. The old road eastwards from the bridge was closed in 1973, when work began on the 07/25 runway of Edinburgh Airport.

High Street, Kirkliston - the 'Lyons Tea' sign is at the door of Rarity's newsagents shop. On the pavement outside the shop can be seen one of the public drinking wells common to all communities before the 1950s. The housing on the right hand side was demolished in 1956 and the house facing towards the camera was demolished when the road was widened in the early 1970s to accommodate buses which were re-routed because of the closure of the A9 at Boathouse Bridge.

This view, taken in about 1906, shows Station Road with its many trees. The thatched cottage on the left (opposite what is now the council office) was the home of the Rarity family. The building with pantiles was on the site of the present-day library.

STATION ROAD KIRKLISTON.

Station Road, about 1910. The small girl in the white dress outside the white cottage is Bella Allen. Church View (nos 39-47) is one of the few three-storey buildings in the community, though the distillery houses on Path Brae (see below) were on three storeys. The slate-roofed cottage nearest the camera was demolished before the First World War and the site was empty until the mid-1980s when a modern pantile-roofed bungalow was built. In the intervening years it was used as garden ground, mainly for the production of vegetables, but with shrubs and flowers next to the pavement, providing a picturesque break in the building line.

After the First World War, three blocks of flats were built on the south side of Path Brae. They were built mainly to house the large distillery workforce (more than 200) in better quality conditions than had hitherto been available. This picture from the 1930s shows the blocks decorated for the Children's Gala. They were demolished in the 1960s - a period of massive municipal destruction nationwide - and in the 1970s a government training scheme enabled the site to be landscaped with its now rapidly maturing trees and shrubs providing a pleasant open vista to travellers arriving from the south.

View south down Station Road pre-1935 and before Almondside was built. On the left, the two-storey building housed Linn's shop at No. 9. Jack Linn ran a coal merchant's business from the rear of the premises. He also rented space at the station where bulk deliveries of coal were stored. The shop was run by his sisters, Liz and Kate. They sold groceries, sweets and everyday hardware such as paraffin, gas mantles and kindling.

Parks foreman, Bill Ritchie, at the wheel of his van in Allison Park prior to local government reorganisation in 1975 when Kirkliston was still part of West Lothian.

10, Downing Street,
Whitehall.

Dear Mr Masterton

I want, from my heart to thank you all for the gift you have sent me for my Red Cross "Aid to Russia" Fund.

From all over the country similar donations are reaching me. I feel they are particularly significant because they shew the continued & intense concern of the citizens of Great Britain for the glorious struggle for

A letter in 1943 from Clementine Churchill, wife of the Prime Minister, to Mr Masterton, landlord of the Newbridge Inn, where a collection for Red Cross aid to the Soviet Union had been made.

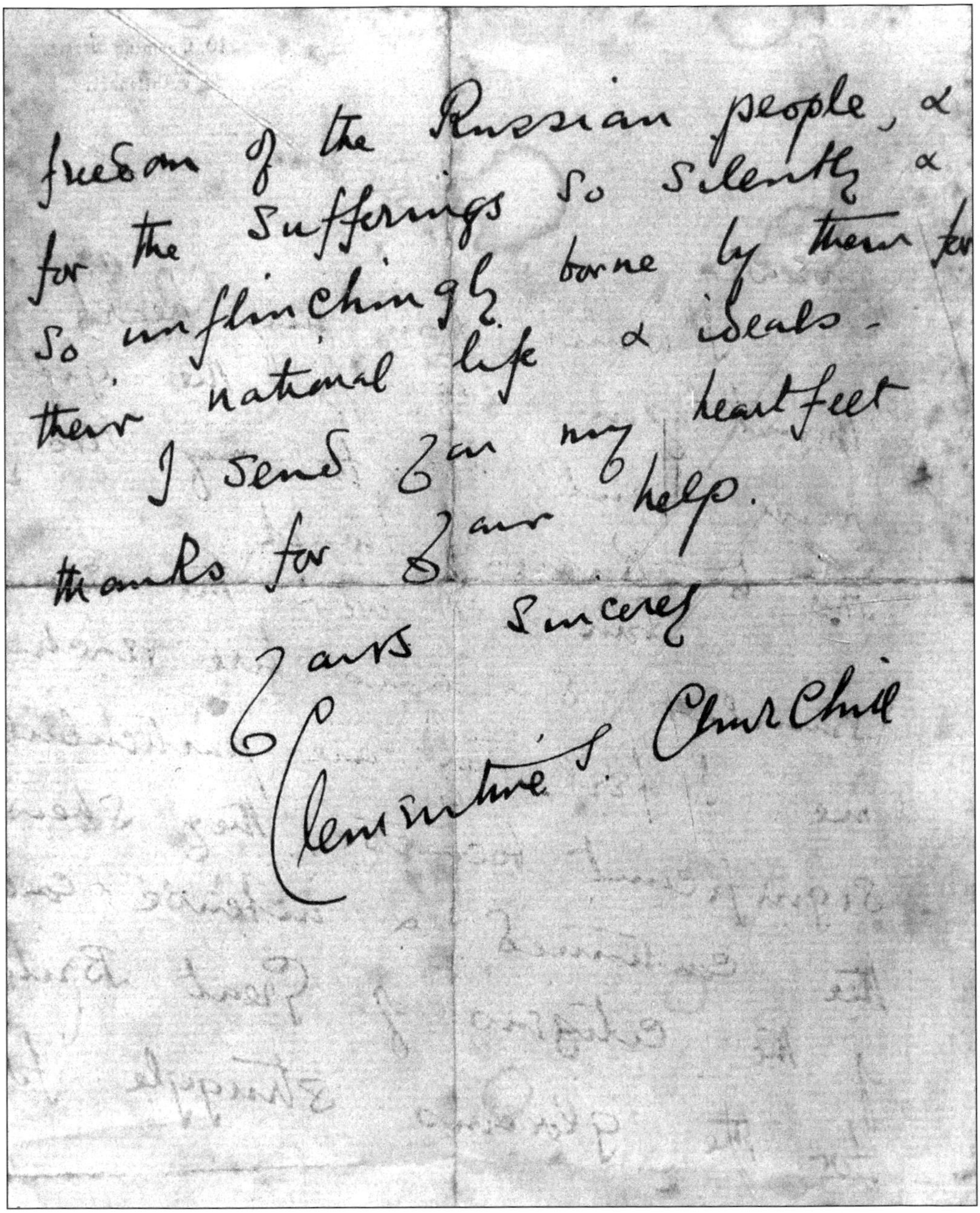

freedom of the Russian people, &
for the sufferings so silently &
so unflinchingly borne by them for
their national life & ideals.

I send you my heartfelt
thanks for your help.

Yours sincerely

Clementine S Churchill

The Newbridge Inn was originally built in 1683 although there have been many alterations since. It was an important and much-welcomed staging post on the journey between Edinburgh and Glasgow. It is pictured here in 1862. The picture below, taken at the same period, also shows Bridge Street, leading to the 'new bridge' over the River Almond.

The interior of the Newbridge Inn in 1943 during the collection for the Red Cross Fund referred to on page 14. Note the poster advertising a gymkhana to be held at Home Farm in June - even during wartime everyday leisure activities took place.

This picture, taken about 1900, shows houses at the foot of Path Brae known as 'Herring Raw and the Ark', mentioned in a poem about a flood written by local poet John McKean (1863-1940). These houses were demolished in order to build the brick distillery houses on Path Brae.

Newliston House was completed in 1793 to plans by Robert Adam (1728-93) who did not live to see it completed. The site was selected before 1747 by the second Earl of Stair who laid out the estate. Plans prepared by William Adam seem to have influenced his son Robert, and probably also David Bryce, who directed the building of the wings in about 1845.

The Hog family bought the Newliston estate in 1753. This is the Hog emblem on top of a pillar at the gates of Newliston House.

Carlowrie House was built in 1851-2 for Thomas Hutchison, merchant and Provost of Leith, who had acquired the estate from David Falconer in 1850. It was built in the Scots Baronial style to a design by David Rhind. The Hutchison family's links with the house and the community ended when the last of the Kirkliston branch of the family, Dr Isobel Hutchison, died in 1982. The house is now occupied by the family of Wilson Marshall of the Marshall Food Group.

Station Road, looking north, before 1936. The most obvious difference from today's view is the presence of so many trees. Sadly, all that survived into the modern era were removed to accommodate the widened roadway in the early 1970s.

Looking westwards along the High Street, about 1910. The cottages on the right were known as Station Terrace, a name recently brought back into use. The wall with the railing on it is still there and can be seen on the left when approaching the Barratt housing estate in the old station yard.

The West Lodge, Dundas Estate. It is otherwise known as the White Lodge and lies between Westfield and Echline. It has recently been renovated.

Marandola's ice cream and chip shops. These shops were situated on the north-west corner at the Toll and were ideally sited for business, being central to the village and lying on the A9 trunk road from Edinburgh to Stirling. For many people from Winchburgh and other nearby settlements a walk to the crossroads at Kirkliston was well worthwhile with the promise of an ice cream at the end. Willie Marandola arrived in Kirkliston from Italy with his family in 1912. They walked from Ratho Station, pushing a cart carrying their belongings. His son Ernest managed the ice cream shop and daughter Theresa the chip shop. They manufactured their own ice cream, in later years a fleet of vans carried Marandola's ice cream throughout east central Scotland. Some of the images in this publication were taken by Alex Marandola, who was a very keen photographer and movie maker.

Christianity came to the area before the sixth century, a monastery having been established at Abercorn before this time. The present parish church building (seen here from the Old Manse in the nineteenth century) dates from Norman times. The structure has seen many alterations over the years to accommodate the increase in worshippers; twice in the eighteen hundreds. In 1822 the heritors seriously considered a proposal to demolish the then existing building and replace it with a larger one! Fortunately for succeeding generations they restricted themselves to an extension to the north, an extension which was enlarged in 1884. In 1843 came the Disruption in the Scottish Church and a second place of worship, the Free Church, was built in High Street, a hundred yards from the parish church. A new manse was built to accommodate the first minister, the Revd James Burns, and his family. The parish church is unusual in that the congregation now faces south, as the north aisle extension of 1822 required a change of seating arrangements from the more normal east-facing configuration.

The south door of the parish church print from Sir Walter Scott's *Provincial Antiquities of Scotland*, published in 1822.

Kirkliston parish church - the pulpit area was altered during the ministry of George Irving, 1965-69. Previously the pipe organ was situated to the right side and the stair to the pulpit on the left. The organ was moved to the west gallery and the dais was constructed. The pulpit is notable for its arcading, appropriate for the Norman-style building. The communion table was gifted in 1927 by the Dudgeon family who had tenanted Almondhill Farm, and now own Humbie Farm.

Hammermen's emblems on a stone in the Kirkyard. All workers in metal could be admitted to the Incorporations of Hammermen in the Scottish burghs on completion of an 'essay', a sample of the work to be done.

Another interesting stone has a headpiece with sculptured heads at either end wearing spectacles. This is an early example, which attracted the attention of the National Science Museum in Kensington.

The Free Church of Scotland pictured in its Jubilee Year of 1893. The church was built in 1843 soon after the Disruption in the Scottish Church. The foundation stone was laid on 4 August 1843 by Dr Thomas Chalmers, leader of the dissidents and the church was formally opened for public worship on 30 September of that year. At the bottom right can be seen the lamp-topped wrought iron arch at the entrance to the Marshall Well, gifted to the community by Robert Marshall of Gateside Farm. He was a noted local philanthropist and left money for poor relief and promotion of education. Bursaries were provided for boys to attend the Royal High School in Edinburgh, as well as educational awards for girls.

A model of the parish church made between 1859 and 1884, when the building was altered and extended. The model, kept in the church, is much in need of restoration.

The manse pictured here was built between 1849 and 1851 for the Free Church ministers. The first to take up residence was Revd James Chalmers Burns who had lived at Milrig after his induction on 30 September 1843, just a few months after the Disruption in the Scottish Church. The congregation was reunited with that of the Established Church in 1929, but while there were two ministers, two groups of parishioners continued to worship separately; the Free Church (United Free from 1900) was allotted the area south of the River Almond and was renamed the Newliston Church; the manse became known as the Newliston manse. The minister of the established church, Revd Robert Maclean, lived in what became known as the Old Manse in Manse Road. After Maclean's death in 1942 the two groups reunited under the Revd William Maxwell. The Newliston Church became the church hall and in recent times has been extended and refurbished to form the Thomas Chalmers Centre. The above photograph dates from about 1870 and the one below from 1994.

Kirkliston's three cemeteries are all grouped around the church. The one pictured here, now known as the old cemetery, as opposed to the churchyard and the new cemetery, was opened in 1875. The picture above shows the old cemetery in 1895 and the one below in 1997.

Jamieson Cottage, 10 Newliston Road. This cottage, built in the early years of the twentieth century, was owned for many years by the Society for Teaching the Blind to Read and used by them as a holiday home. This photograph was taken on the occasion of a visit by the house committee in July 1913 and shows the house, garden, two guests and the matron.

Station House was built in 1916 to house the Station Agent and his family. In 1965, as a result of the Beeching cuts, the railway here ceased to exist. The last agent, Henry Henderson, remained in the house until his death in 1978. British Rail sold the property to its present owners in 1980 and they extended it and took up residence in 1982. The former railway is now a very popular walkway from Newbridge to Queensferry and many walkers, cyclists and horse riders will recognise this house with its distinctive mansard roof.

One of the few visible antiquities in the parish is the Catstane, now situated within Edinburgh Airport's boundaries. It lies very close to Boathouse Bridge. It is seen here being examined by local historian Donald Whyte. The inscription reads:

IN OC TV
MVLO JACIT
VETTA F
VICTI.

This may be freely translated as 'IN THIS MOUND LIES VETTA SON OF VICTI.'
Excavation and examination of a number of nearby stone kists was carried out a number of years ago and the results of the research published.

Looking southwards down Queensferry Road. The steel houses on the left were built in 1927. Some have now been clad in brick. Very little has changed in this street, apart from the loss of some trees and telegraph poles. Note the lack of vehicles.

Kirkliston from the River Almond. This postcard, sent from Kirkliston to Newcastle on Tyne, is postmarked 3 Jan 1905.

The South Lodge, Dundas Estate, as seen on a postcard bought by a sailor serving on HMS *Ramilles* in 1918. The view is just recognisable today, though now the road is the main link from the Edinburgh-Glasgow motorway to the Forth Road Bridge and hence is extremely busy with traffic.

Castle House at 25-27 High Street. The inscription over the door reads '1682 IF/ID'. The initials refer to John Finland and Janet Dick. Robert Burns and William Nicol (Latin master at the High School of Edinburgh) stopped here on 24 August 1787 at the start of their Highland tour. The mites must have bothered the bard, as he cut the following lines on a pane of glass -

'The ants about their clod employ their care,
And think the business of the world is theirs;
Lo: Waxen combs seem palaces to bees,
And mites conceive the world to be a cheese.'

Unfortunately, the window pane was sold many years ago and is believed to be in Vancouver, Canada. The final word of the verse may be the origin of the village's nickname 'Cheesetown'. The house was for many years in the ownership of the Stephens family and in addition to domestic accommodation a small licensed grocers was run on the ground floor. Miners on their way home from the shale pit at Ingliston would often stop for a 'hauf' to revive them after a hard day's toil. After the last of the local Stephens died, the house was sold to the Wardells who renovated and restored what had sadly become a very dilapidated building.

From small beginnings at Ratho Station in 1879, where it established its headquarters, the Hillwood Cooperative Society expanded to branches at Kirkliston, South Queensferry, Ratho and Balerno. The Society merged with St Cuthbert's Cooperative Society (founded in Edinburgh in 1859) in 1966 and in 1981 St Cuthbert's was absorbed by the Scottish Midland Cooperative Society - Scotmid.

The former Maitland telephone exchange. This was an automated unmanned facility and was closed in 1973. Since then it has been used as a store.

The war memorial at the Cross, showing the signs for the A9, until 1972 the main trunk road from Edinburgh to Stirling. This main road, running east to west through the village, has now been 'de-trunked', though it seems to carry as much traffic as it ever did.

The War Memorial, sited on the north eastern corner of the Toll, to the fallen in the two World Wars. This face shows the names of the private soldiers from the parish who fell in the Great War of 1914-1918.

PRIVATES

WILLIAM AITKEN	JAMES LILLIE
GEORGE ALLAN	GEORGE MACPHERSON
JAMES ARBUCKLE	ROBERT G. MACPHERSON
JOHN BEGBIE	JAMES McFARLANE
WALTER BENNIE	ROBERT MEIKLE
GEORGE BINNIE	ROBERT NICOL
GEORGE BORTHWICK	JAMES O'NEILL
THOMAS BORTHWICK	JAMES PATERSON, GNr.
NORMAN CAMPBELL	JAMES PATERSON
SCOTT CAMPBELL	JAMES PROVEN
JAMES CHESSAR	ANDREW RAMAGE
ANDREW E. CHESSAR	WILLIAM REEDER
PETER ERSKINE	JAMES REEDER
ABRAHAM FOY	ROBERT REID
JAMES FOY	PETER D. ROBERTSON
DAVID J. FRAME	JAMES SHANKS
JAMES GARDNER	JAMES SMITH
JAMES GREER	GEORGE STEWART
WILLIAM GREIG	JOHN D. SUTHERLAND
GEORGE PAUL HOGG	PETER TAYLOR
WILLIAM HOGG	JOHN WEDDELL
DAVID HOPE	JAMES WEIR

The pair of shops referred to elsewhere in connection with the Marandola family. The ice cream parlour is now a Chinese takeaway restaurant and the chip shop a video store. The modern pace of change is so rapid that the day after this photograph was taken (in 1997) 'Silver Screen Video' had gone, to be replaced by 'Movie Express.'

A national postal service was introduced by the government in 1790. This building at No. 11 Main Street housed the Post Office for well over a century and in 1974 the business moved across the street to No. 66. No. 11 is now a dwelling house.

Hallyards Castle was built in the seventeenth century for John Skene. The mansion house was built on the site of the old manor of the Knights of St John and stood for many years. By the end of the First World War it was a ruin (pictured here) and with the underground workings of the Ingliston Shale Mine causing subsidence, the house was demolished in the late 1920s.

Foxhall. The estate and house have been in the ownership of the Gammell family since 1964 and the land used as a tree and plant nursery. The most prominent owner this century was Lt Col John Cadell (1862-1942), in whose son's memory a church hall was built in Newbridge. The house was used during the Second World War as a hostel for members of the Women's Land Army.

The Old Toll House. Tolls were levied for the upkeep of the turnpike road. The 'lollipop man' is Willie Aitchison, at one time village postman. His family lived at Ashton Cottage in Station Road (now named Station Cottage). His daughter, Liza, was secretary to Baron Wheatley of Shettleston, former judge at the High Court in Edinburgh.

Toddshill Road, part of the Manse Road housing scheme, the first major local housing development after the Second World War. This scheme was built in the early 1950s by West Lothian County Council; a large percentage is now owner-occupied as residents have taken advantage of the 'right-to-buy' legislation.

New housing development flourished in the 1960s and 70s with this council scheme in The Glebe, another on Gateside Farm and private developments on Almondhill and Newmains Farms. In 1965, before a suitable grating was fitted to the drain designed to take the water of the Mains Burn and other surface water, severe flooding was experienced. It may have worried prospective tenants, but was great fun for the kids!

Building on a large scale ceased after the boom years of the 1960s and 70s. Subsequent building was largely confined to small infill sites; the 1990s have seen another boom. Land at Station Road and behind the Newliston Arms was used to site amenity flats and a new library to replace the 'temporary' structure built in 1974, which in turn replaced the leaky mobile library. The new library, seen here, has five flats above it.

Some of the new amenity flats on the corner of Station Road and High Street. Traditional Scottish features such as the external staircase tower have been used in the design of these buildings which were completed in 1996.

So many objections were raised in 1982, when Hopetoun Estates sought planning permission to build up to 900 houses on the remains of Newmains Farm, that a public enquiry was held. The outcome was refusal at that time. Come the 1990s, and the concept of 'planning gain', permission was granted for 140 houses and a leisure centre, shown here, with the high embankment of the motorway spur from the M9 to the Forth Road Bridge in the background.

Part of the new housing estate at Kirklands Park, still being built in 1998. At the time the first houses were being built the City of Edinburgh Council had a policy of not naming streets after people. This has now changed, as some of the streets have been named after Alexander Glendinning, a former tenant of Newmains Farm, where these houses are sited.

Fields on the farms all had names. The new houses, built by Walker Homes, are all in the one called 'Malachi', so named because it was always the last field to be ploughed, mown, harvested, etc (Malachi is the last book of the Old Testament).

Before the advent of street names and numbers, all houses were named. Here we have Sunnybank in Station Road, which started life as a single-storey cottage in the nineteenth century. It was extended upwards and divided into four dwellings at the height of the shale oil boom. In living memory, No. 23 (the rear part of the ground floor) housed a family of thirteen in two rooms, with an outside toilet and washhouse. On the left can be seen the council and registrar's office, which once was the headquarters of Kirkliston & Winchburgh District Council.

Lochend Cottages at the junction of Lochend Road and the Glasgow Road. They were built in the latter part of the nineteenth century probably to house shale miners and their families. Despite many alterations they are still recognisable today. This photograph dates from the 1920s before Glasgow Road was made a dual carriageway.

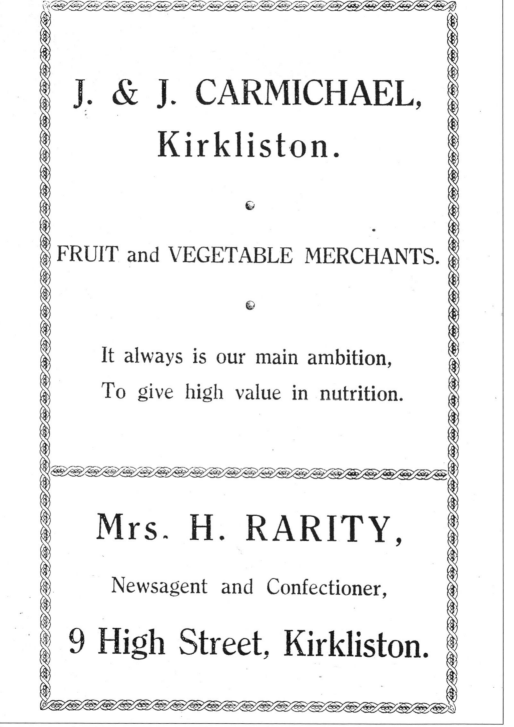

J. & J. CARMICHAEL,
Kirkliston.

FRUIT and VEGETABLE MERCHANTS.

It always is our main ambition,
To give high value in nutrition.

Mrs. H. RARITY,

Newsagent and Confectioner,

9 High Street, Kirkliston.

Then as now, local organisations sought sponsorship and support from local businesses. This page and the one following show advertisements taken by local traders in *Kirkliston Echoes*, a fund-raising booklet published in 1926.

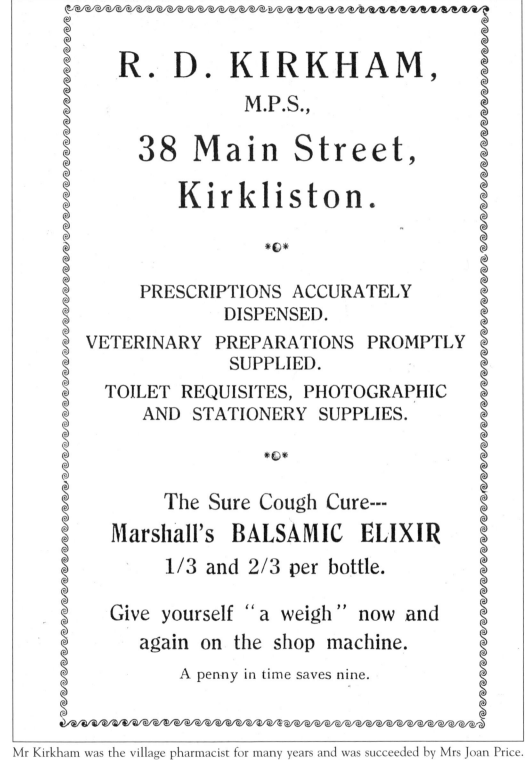

R. D. KIRKHAM,

M.P.S.,

38 Main Street, Kirkliston.

☯

PRESCRIPTIONS ACCURATELY
DISPENSED.

VETERINARY PREPARATIONS PROMPTLY
SUPPLIED.

TOILET REQUISITES, PHOTOGRAPHIC
AND STATIONERY SUPPLIES.

☯

The Sure Cough Cure---
Marshall's BALSAMIC ELIXIR
1/3 and 2/3 per bottle.

Give yourself "a weigh" now and
again on the shop machine.

A penny in time saves nine.

Mr Kirkham was the village pharmacist for many years and was succeeded by Mrs Joan Price.
When she retired, the current 'chemist', Mr W.C. Jones, took over the business.

Dundas Castle and its environs used to play an important part in the lives of the villagers. Many took advantage of the freedom of access granted by the owner to use the beautiful grounds for Sunday walks and many fund-raising events were held there, as can be seen from this poster. The photograph below illustrates such an event, with the mansion house in the background.

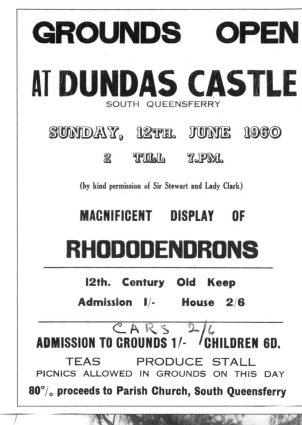

GROUNDS OPEN

AT DUNDAS CASTLE
SOUTH QUEENSFERRY

SUNDAY, 12TH. JUNE 1960
2 TILL 7.PM.

(by kind permission of Sir Stewart and Lady Clark)

MAGNIFICENT DISPLAY OF

RHODODENDRONS

12th. Century Old Keep

Admission 1/- House 2/6

CARS 2/6

ADMISSION TO GROUNDS 1/- CHILDREN 6D.

TEAS PRODUCE STALL

PICNICS ALLOWED IN GROUNDS ON THIS DAY

80°/₀ proceeds to Parish Church, South Queensferry

Newliston House has many attractive dwellings in its grounds. Here is the East lodge, familiar to many local residents, lying adjacent to Milrig farm on Newliston Road.

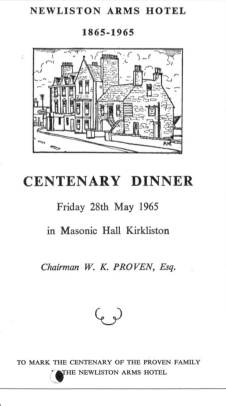

NEWLISTON ARMS HOTEL

1865-1965

CENTENARY DINNER

Friday 28th May 1965

in Masonic Hall Kirkliston

Chairman W. K. PROVEN, Esq.

TO MARK THE CENTENARY OF THE PROVEN FAMILY
THE NEWLISTON ARMS HOTEL

The Newliston Arms Hotel was owned and managed by the Proven family for over a hundred years. A centenary dinner was held, addressed by, among others, William Merrilees, OBE, Chief Constable.

44

Two

The Land

Kirkliston prior to the Industrial Revolution depended for many centuries on the farming industry for its livelihood. Village people worked both on the land and in the farmhouses as domestic servants. Businesses such as saddlers, blacksmiths, builders, joiners, wheelwrights etc. thrived; and on those businesses were built the services and shops to serve the population. The farms were largely tenanted, being owned by the three main estates, Newliston, Hopetoun and Dundas. All the land that the built-up area of the village now occupies was once in the ownership of the great estates. Farming is still a major activity locally, though the numbers employed to run the farms have virtually gone. A farm which fifty years ago employed twenty is now run by two with the occasional help of contractors at harvest time.

Linlithgow Young Farmers' Club outing to Almondhill Farm. Second from left is William Allison Jr, farmer, and third from left is John Whyte, a cattleman at Almondhill from 1941-1973.

Gateside Farm, then occupied (c.1955) by Tom Clark, lay on the old highway between Kirkliston and Winchburgh (via Lindsay's Craigs, Overton and Ross's Wood). It was lost when West Lothian County Council acquired the land on which to build 226 houses. The steading was demolished about 1960. The housing scheme which was built on the farm has some historic street names - Cotlaws, King Edward's Way, Maitland Hog Lane and Cleric's Hill.

Not in Bonnie Strathyre, but at Breastmill, Kirkliston! The story goes that Thomas Scott, the miller (shown here) was given two calves in payment of a debt, and grazed them in the little field between the Niddry Burn (known locally as Tam Scott's Burn) and the approach to Maitland Bridge. He was so kind to them that their growth was prodigious and he was forced to sell them.

Humbie Farm, 1950. A piece of ground that had been used for potato pits is brought under the plough late and sown in grain by hand. The men with the sowing sheets are on the left Rob Ballantyne, a ploughman, and on the right, Bob Robertson, the farm grieve. In the background can be seen the farmhouse.

The horse was for many centuries the primary motive force on farms, tractors becoming more common only after the Second World War and even then only slowly. This picture shows the ploughman and his team at work on Wheatlands Farm about 1930.

Agricultural shows were highlights in the lives of most farm workers and one of the main attractions, then as now, was the heavy horses groomed and dressed in their finery. Here is shown a prize-winning dressed horse from Humbie Farm at Linlithgow Agricultural Show in 1953. The men are Donald Whyte and his assistant William Hope.

The Royal Highland and Agricultural Society of Scotland

June 21, 22, 23 and 24   121

EDINBURGH SHOW 1955   **SEASON TICKET**   EDINBURGH SHOW 1955

£1 : 10s.

THIS TICKET IS NOT TRANSFERABLE

R. M. LEMMON, Secretary

Admit MISS ISOBEL G. YOUNG.

The Annual Show of the Royal Highland and Agricultural Society of Scotland was (and continues to be) the acme of all the shows. Each year saw a different venue as the show moved throughout Scotland. Now it has a permanent home at Ingliston in the grounds of Ingliston House, also home to a motor racing circuit. Many permanent buildings have been erected, including a large exhibition hall.

This image is of the 'Best in Show' in 1955. It was not a local entry, the decoration being in the style used north of the Firth of Forth.

Harvest time is always a busy period on the farm. Here are Jock Whyte, Jock McCabe and Dick the horse at harvest on Almondhill Farm in 1950.

The days when fields were full of 'haystacks' after harvest are long gone. Mechanisation has changed the face of agriculture - in this picture are three carts, two horses and six people, stacking wheat straw in the 1950s.

Grain is now all cut by combine harvester, but as late as the 1960s the binder was at work, and the grain was stacked. Seen here are the signs of the demise of the horse as a working animal - this small Massey-Ferguson tractor could do the work of several. The man on the stack is David Seaton and on the trailer, forking sheaves, is William Robertson

Almondhill Farm, 1948. The occasion is clearly a visit by a delegation from a Commonwealth country, accompanied by a Scottish Office official. The lady is Jean Cockburn, who received a silver medal for thirty years service, then a gold one for fifty years. She served with Edward Dudgeon before William Allison took over the tenancy in 1926. She worked long after normal retirement age. In the background is Davy Smith, the farm grieve.

The Stepping Stones, Almond River, Kirkliston

The River Almond formed the boundary between West Lothian and Midlothian. On the other side of the river from the village lay the shale mine at Ingliston. In order to reach work the miners from the village had to cross the river and they did this by means of the stepping stones near Hallyards farm. The stones are seen here about 1900.

Fed up with wet feet and the uncertainty of the men getting to work, the community organised a public subscription to raise money to build a bridge over the river. This bridge (known as the Miners' Brig) was built in 1907 by Redpath Brown and opened in May of that year; the stones were later removed (about 1932) to alleviate flooding. Ingliston Shale Mine was active from 1891-1926.

The bridge was inspected, declared unsafe and closed in 1980. After a concerted campaign led by the Community Council, the local authority, then the City of Edinburgh District Council, organised and financed its replacement. The new bridge was opened in 1989.

As can be seen from the first picture in this series, the stepping stones were a popular place for the local population. Here are Bruce Simpson and his father in 1932 enjoying the sunshine.

A detail of the 'Miners' Brig' taken about 1960 before its closure and eventual replacement.

Being in central Scotland and so close to many communication channels, the modernisation and upgrading of transport infrastructure inevitably affects the village. Here is the Milrig bridge, over the newly-diverted River Almond, under construction in 1969 as part of the M9 motorway.

The last harvest in the field of Newmains Farm to the west of Queensferry Road before the construction of the first phase of Wimpey housing in the mid-1960s. The roofline of the steel houses in Queensferry Road can just be seen.

A pen and ink view of the village from the south drawn by James Maitland Hog sometime between 1843 and 1858. The Free Church spire was added in 1880 as a memorial to him.

Vertical aerial view of the village and the surrounding countryside in 1947. None of the 'modern' development of the village has yet taken place, with the first post-war housing being built to the west of Manse Road in the 1950s. On the top right is Almondhill Farm, with the farmhouse almost surrounded by trees and on the left edge, just to the north of the Stirling Road, lies Newmains Farm. So much housing has now been built on the farmland that neither farm is any longer viable.

Three

Industry and Commerce

For many centuries the only industry was farming and its support in the building, tool and horse trades. However the eighteenth and nineteenth centuries brought the Industrial Revolution and with it society's greater needs for infrastructure. First came the canals and railways, then great improvements in the trunk roads, all mainly for the movement of goods. Kirkliston first had its distillery by 1800, the Union Canal at nearby Ratho in 1820, the Edinburgh-Glasgow railway in 1842, its own railway line in 1865, the Forth Bridge in 1890 and the shale oil mines from the mid-1800s to the mid-1900s when this industry failed. We also have Edinburgh International Airport on our doorstep. In more modern times the infrastructure has attracted many more industries to the area, including electronic, computer and communication. All this has resulted in population migration and growth industries.

The Edinburgh to Glasgow railway was opened in 1842. Ratho Station was the nearest halt to Kirkliston. In 1863 the Edinburgh & Glasgow Railway Company constructed a line between Ratho Station and South Queensferry with an intermediate station at Kirkliston. In 1866 the local station was opened. Kirkliston Station had a life span of 100 years. It closed to passenger traffic in 1930 but remained a goods station for another thirty years. It was closed in 1966. The line has been converted to a walkway. Above is a general view of Kirkliston Station looking south-west. Note, in the middle left, there is a gauge for checking loads to ensure safe passage through tunnels and bridges. Below is the station building.

Kirkliston lost its regular passenger service on 22 September 1930. The engine *Glen Douglas* visited with specials on 12 June 1960 (illustrated) and 13 April 1963.

Engine No. 80114 pulling out of Kirkliston on 23 June 1963 towards Forth Bridge. On the right of the photograph is the Burnshot Road. Note the old fashioned road sign.

Gates closed at the level crossing in Wellflats Road to allow passage of a goods train out of the station yard. The line where the gates are open to allow the passage of traffic is the distillery siding. The engine shown here is *Maude*, the local shunter. This engine still operates at the Scottish Railway Preservation Society's line at Bo'ness. The picture below shows a goods train rolling through the station, *c.*1960.

The North British Railway Company - passenger service between Edinburgh and Dunfermline commenced 5 March 1890. Note that the Queensferry Passage amended its service on the opening of the bridge.

'Kirkliston Turkish Baths?' - No! Mae Marandola at work making ice cream in Marandola's factory in East Main Street for distribution locally or for consumption at the ice cream parlour.

A Marandola ice cream van, c.1960. The family at that time had a small fleet of vans which served the surrounding area, covering Winchburgh, Broxburn, Ratho, Currie and Balerno, as well as the western suburbs of Edinburgh.

Marandola's ice cream van fleet - note the variety of vehicles that had been customised to get the ice cream to the local folks.

Outside the smithy in Newliston Road in the early years of the twentieth century. An apprentice is shoeing a horse as Robert Lawson, James Lawson (senior) and James Lawson (grandfather) look on. The smithy is still in existence today although no longer in use because last smith, also James Lawson, has retired.

Jim Lawson at work on a section of wrought iron work in the smithy. Jim often entered his work in competitions such as the Royal Highland Show at nearby Ingliston and met with considerable success.

Breastmill seen from the Newliston Manse, c. 1890. Note that Breastmill House was then a single-storey building. As was the practice at that time, when extra accommodation was required, houses were extended upwards - Breastmill House is now a two-storey building.

There has been a grist mill here since the sixteenth century. It belonged to the Dundas family until 1723 when it was purchased by the Earl of Stair. From 1863 until its closure in 1928, it was run by the Scott family. The last miller was Tam Scott. His daughter Betty married Tom Wilson, the GP who succeeded Dr Stewart after the Second World War.

After its closure in 1928, Breastmill lay derelict until it was restored as a dwelling house in 1967/68.

Priestmill.

View of Breastmill (sometimes known as 'Priestmill') - from the manse garden. A Water colour by Susan Robertson Burns (daughter of Revd James Burns - minister of the Free Church in Kirkliston). She died in 1914.

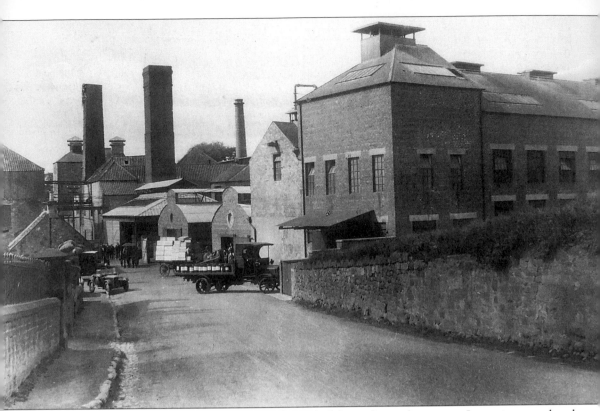

A distillery has been in existence since the end of the eighteenth century. It was improved and enlarged in 1825 and in 1878 it was aquired by Distillers Company Limited. Ten years later their annual output was 700,000 gallons of malt and grain whisky. In 1914 fire destroyed most of the stills and it was after this time that malt extract production started as the stills were not replaced. Distillers Company Limited owned the distillery until 1986 when the company was taken over by Guinness plc to become United Distillers. The new owners promptly sold the buildings and closed the business. They also closed and sold off the United Yeast Company, a food distribution subsidiary occupying a modern warehouse and offices at the rear. The site is now used by a company producing malt and home brew kits, a small printing business and the warehouse is occupied by Scotmid Cooperative Society.

An idyllic view of the distillery reservoir. Water was necessary in large quantities for the distillery and was supplied from two sources above the works, Humbie Reservoir and Pike's Pool in what is now Allison Park.

A group of distillery workers having a break in the Glebe in 1952. They are Mary Mitchell, Annie Ingram, Annie Mabon, Chrissie Gordon, Margaret Reid, Isa Aitken, John Gaffney, Nan Havey and Jean Johnson.

DCL workforce standing outside the distillery in 1938. There is a high number of women amongst them, a proportion which grew larger during the war which followed.

DCL malt extract bottling factory. Note the flypapers hanging from the roof beams. What would environmental health inspectors say about this nowadays one wonders?

A group of engineers and other tradesmen and labourers in 1935. As the company was a major employer in the area, many boys served their apprenticeships in their respective trades here.

DCL pug and crew, *c.* 1938. William Thomson is standing on the footplate and William Hunter is standing in the foreground with a shunter's pole. DCL houses in Path Brae can be seen in the background. The distillery was connected by a siding to Kirkliston station.

A union meeting at the distillery in the 1950s. Addressing the workers is John Kinghorn and amongst his listeners are Bobby Young, David Sorley, Jimmy Arbuckle and Charlie Borthwick.

Ruth Mochrie running up the path at the cottages in Newliston Road adjacent to the distillery, c. 1962. In the background can be seen railway wagons on the distillery's own siding.

Two illustrations of Kirkliston distillery from *Whisky Distilleries of the United Kingdom* by Alfred Barnard, published in 1887. As well as a detailed description of the works itself, comment was made on the 'environmental friendliness' of the manager who, instead of discharging the waste into the nearby river Almond, pumped the liquid by pipe to South Queensferry and used the solid residue to feed a large number of pigs kept at the distillery, pigs which won many prizes at agricultural shows across Scotland.

A group of miners from Whitequarries Shale Mine, owned by Scottish Oils. From the 1930s to the 1960s the mine supplied shale to Winchburgh via an electric railway. The mine's workings extended under the River Forth.

More shale mining in the environs of Kirkliston which provided employment in the area. Pictured here are a group of miners at the Newliston Shale Mine at the end of the nineteenth century.

An airport, both military and civilian, has existed at nearby Turnhouse since 1915. The passenger terminal at Turnhouse, shown above, *c.* 1970, was replaced soon afterwards with a brand new building at Ingliston, shown below, *c.* 1990. There soon followed a new runway (after a long and bitterly-fought public enquiry) and the airport now boasts the most modern of facilities, lacking only a rail link.

The Drambuie Liqueur Company opened a new plant on the west side of Kirkliston in 1969. As they disposed of various small sites in Edinburgh, more space was required, and a major extension was added to the Kirkliston works in 1987. All blending and bottling for the world-famous nectar now takes place here, much of it exported. Above is the building in 1969 and below the extension of 1987.

Four

Education

Kirkliston appears to have had a schoolmaster before 1648. Prior to the Education Act of 1872 what education existed was largely undertaken by the churches and some private 'adventure' schools. The school at Loanhead in Queensferry Road was originally erected by the Free Church but was taken over by the parochial board in 1873. The clock on the gable was erected in 1912 in memory of Alexander Glendinning, tenant of Newmains Farm and chairman of the school board for some time. The education system was one of the few ways of monitoring the health of the population in the early part of the century, regular examinations of the children being carried out by the Medical Officer of Health. Epidemic illnesses such as measles, scarlet fever, diphtheria, whooping cough and mumps were common and the school was closed sometimes for weeks at a time for health reasons. In 1974 the new primary school was opened at the west end of the village when the old school became overcrowded. The old school in Queensferry Road is still in use as a nursery school and community centre.

A view of the old primary school showing the Glendinning clock on the gable and a surprisingly traffic free Queensferry Road.

Children leaving the old primary school in Queensferry Road, *c.* 1960. The old outside toilet block can be seen in the background. No inside toilets in the 'good old days!'

Many will remember the public drinking wells which were found scattered around the urban areas of our towns and cities - the great drive for public health through the provision of clean, safe drinking water had a very public face. Kirkliston was no exception. Every school playground had one so the children could refresh themselves while at play. No school shops with sugar-rich fizzy drinks in those days! This picture dates from the 1950s. In the background can be seen part of Loanhead House.

No school does without its class photographs. The following pages have a selection from which many faces will be recognised. The one above dates from before the First World War and is unfortunately too early for any now to be identified.

Lochend School, Ratho Station

As well as the school in Kirkliston, one was also built at Lochend to accommodate the children of families living south of the River Almond at Hallyards, Newbridge and Ratho Station. Built in 1890, with later additions, it was closed in 1975 when the new runway at Edinburgh Airport was opened for use. Noise levels were such (the threshold of the new airstrip being less than 500 feet away) that a new school was required, and one was built at Norwood in Ratho Station. After 1975 the building was used, amongst other things, as a candle factory. It became so dilapidated that it was demolished in 1992.

Rewards for educational achievement are no new thing. Here is a certificate of merit awarded in 1919 to one of Newbridge School's star pupils, Miss Mary McDonald.

Kirkliston Primary School, 1937. Some faces should still be recognised: among them are Archie Erskine (second from right, back row), Billy Allison (fourth from right, back row), Nan Havey (seventh from left, middle row) with Kitty Anderson on her left.

Class photograph, 1950.

One of the last photographs taken of a class at the school in Queensferry Road in 1972. Later that year the school occupied the new building at Carmel Road, beside the newly opened Drambuie bottling facility.

The new school in 1986. This building has had a troubled history of a leaking roof - shortly after this picture was taken the school had a new roof installed. The same thing is about to happen again (1998) which says something about the quality of design and maintenance of public buildings of this era.

A familiar sight - the school crossing patrol or 'lollipop man'. This is Mathie Arbuckle in 1959.

The Marshall Well was presented to the village by Robert Marshall (1790-1875), who tenanted Gateside Farm, but was a clothier in Edinburgh, becoming a Burgess and Guildbrother in 1822. Later he formed a partnership with his apprentice Alexander Aitken and the firm was known as Marshall & Aitken. He presented the well in 1867. Marshall was a benefactor of the bowling club which bore his name for a while. He made many other gifts, including school bursaries. This picture dates from 1893.

Children outside the school in the early part of the twentieth century. Note that many were unshod, boots being expensive. Many children were from the families of poorly-paid farmworkers who often could not afford the luxury of shoes or boots for their offspring, particularly those too young to work at the planting and harvesting.

The school staff, pictured, *c.* 1914. Amongst them are Mr Peter Munnoch, headmaster, Miss Alexina Masson Grieve and Miss Jessie Hunter. Miss Hunter taught in the school from 1893 to 1931.

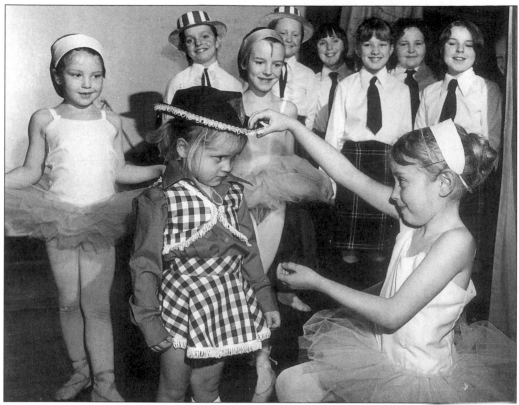

One of the lasting institutions in the village is the Bruce School of Dancing. Mrs Edith Bruce has taught many hundreds of children and adults from the 1970s to present day the skills of ballet and tap dancing, as well as running a multitude of keep fit classes for all ages. Here are some of her pupils displaying their skills.

A group of boys at the old primary school in the mid-1930s. Many of them who still reside locally will recognise themselves and their mates.

Class photograph, *c.* 1960. Centre in the front row is Cathy Robertson, now Mrs Kellett. Second from right in the back row is Billy Robertson. The teacher is Mr Howie.

Before the First World War. A class of non-smiling faces posed at the main door of the schoolhouse. In many ways there wasn't a lot for children to smile about - epidemic illness being common and the necessity for the children of agricultural workers to do hard physical work in the fields, assisting their parents.

Five
Recreation and Leisure

Whether sport, reading, amateur dramatics, walking, a visit to the pub after work or just a gossip on the corner, life would be unbearable without some leisure and something to do with it. Kirkliston is no exception, and runs the full gamut. The community has for many years supported an active bowling club which, as well as sport, provides an important venue for much social life. For children there have been the many uniformed organisations which have included a large element of education and some religion as well as being an organised outlet for youthful energy. Football teams for all ages have existed at one time or another and there have been the inevitable social events associated with the workplace, particularly the distillery which employed many local people in its almost two hundred year history. Seen here are members of the bowling club at the end of the nineteenth century. They are posing with what is probably the Rosebery Cup.

One of the most popular organisations in the village is the Kirkliston branch of the Scottish Old Age Pensioners' Association. As well as monthly socials, entertainments and dinners, in the summer months at least one organised outing takes place. This is one of many bus trips, on this occasion in the 1950s. It was organised by Bella Allen, third from right in the photograph.

Provision of play equipment for children is no new thing. Here is the swing park in Station Road in 1937. The children are mostly from the then newly-built houses in Almondside. Still recognisable is the stone wall, now forming the boundary of the library car park. The hut on the right overlooked the bowling green.

The Brownies are a long-established presence in the community. Here are a group in 1931 pictured with Brown Owl and Tawny Owl in the garden of the Newliston Manse, with the parish church in the background.

Another of the childrens' uniformed groups, along with the Brownies, Guides, Cubs, Scouts and Boys' Brigade, were the Lifeboys, seen here as they appeared in 1936. This organisation no longer exists, though the Sea Scouts do, but alas, without a branch in Kirkliston.

Kirkliston Athletic Football Club, 1928/29. One of the many teams to be formed this club played its matches at Station Park which lay to the south of the Edinburgh Road immediately east of the railway line.

Amongst the organisations for young people the Boys' Brigade has always played a prominent part. Here is their football team in 1928. Many of its members will be recognised, having spent most, if not all of their lives in the village. The middle row, for instance, includes Hugh Cockburn, Alex Marandola, Hugh Forsyth and Sam Brown.

The first bowling club in Kirkliston was formed in 1869. The green was on a small scale having only two rinks. The present club was formed - or rather reconstituted – in 1882, when a clubhouse was erected. For a time it was known as the Marshall Bowling Club after local benefector Robert Marshall (1790-1875), but afterwards reverted to its original name of Kirkliston Bowling Club. It was one of the original clubs of the Linlithgowshire Bowling Association. The game is still popular in the district with clubs at Newbridge (founded in 1906) and Winchburgh. A ladies section was established at Kirkliston in 1996. All the local clubs have had the benefit of keen and dedicated committees, and many trophies have been won.

Music, particularly that of the highland bagpipe, has played an important part in the life of the community, for as well as the annual Armistice Day parade other events such as the Childrens' Gala Day procession require at least one band. Above is the Kirkliston Pipe Band resplendent in its new uniforms in 1947. After this group disbanded, for many years bands had to be imported. However, in 1990 a group of local enthusiasts, with generous sponsorship help from the Drambuie Liqueur Company, established the Kirkliston Drambuie Pipe Band. They are seen below on their inaugural parade on 22 September 1990.

Many pipe bands in Scotland compete in the various championships and the Kirkliston

Drambuie band is no exception. They are pictured here inside the Drambuie building with some of the trophies they have won. Below is a show of the silverware.

A happy group of ladies at a dance in the Masonic Hall in the 1950s. The village has been fortunate in the provision of leisure and meeting facilities - the bowling club, the church hall, the Masonic Hall, the reading room (burned down in the 1930s) and the community centre.

Obviously not a very nice day! A group of Boys' Brigade members (and canine friend) assembled in The Square prior to a walk to raise money for charity in 1971.

An active and popular local organisation has long been the Scottish Womens' Rural Institute. Here are seen some of the members of the Newbridge and Ratho Station Branch on an outing in 1948.

A group of volunteers, under the auspices of the Community Centre Association, established a Lunch Club in the community centre with the aim of enhancing the lives of the housebound. It was a much valued and appreciated resource, relying totally on volunteer effort for transport, food, organisation and entertainment. This picture shows the members and most of the volunteers at the Christmas party in 1980.

The Boys' Brigade, 1st Kirkliston Company, 1891. Most boys in the community were, at one time or another, members. As well as routine parades, religious education, camps and sporting activities, a loyal band of ex-members sprang up and in the 1930s a series of dramatic 'Kinderspiels' were produced with their help. Below is a scene from the SS *Mary Ann*, and, opposite top, one from *The Magic Ruby*, with below it the entire cast. They were very pretty!

Watching sport was just as popular as participating in it. Then as now, football was the most popular of all sports in central Scotland. As well as following the local village teams, support for the major clubs in the Scottish League was plentiful. At international level many will remember the biennial trip to Wembley. Here is a group of Scotland supporters from Kirkliston in Cardiff in 1950 for the international against Wales.

Many companies and businesses held an annual dance. Here are some local members of staff of St Cuthbert's Cooperative Society at their dance at Ingliston in 1965. Amongst them are Nan and Jean Havey, Nan Emslie, Chrissie Stewart, Bill Blain and Bob Kembo.

The Church was once the social hub of the village and in the 1950s a host of groups existed, amongst them the dramatic club, which presented many productions over the years. The cast of Joan Kennedy, Isobel Shand, Tom Graham, Agnes McGowan, Tom Gray, George Barclay, John Murray, John Stewart and John Belmont will be familiar to many.

∴ **KIRKLISTON PARISH CHURCH** ∴

DRAMATIC CLUB
presents

See How They Run

A Farce in Three Acts
by
PHILIP KING

❧

SYNOPSIS OF SCENES

The action takes place in the Hall at the Vicarage,
Merton-cum-Middlewick.

ACT 1. .... An afternoon in September.
ACT 2. .... The same night.
ACT 3. .... A few minutes after Act 2.

CAST

IDA (a maid)	*Joan Kennedy*
MISS SKILLON	*Isobel Shand*
THE REVEREND LIONEL TOOP	*Tom Graham*
PENELOPE TOOP (his Wife)	*Agnes McGowan*
LANCE-CORPORAL CLIVE WINTON	*Tom Gray*
THE INTRUDER	*George Barclay*
THE BISHOP OF LAX	*John Murray*
THE REVEREND ARTHUR HUMPHREY	*John Stewart*
SERGEANT TOWERS	*John Belmont*

❧

Producer . .	ELIZABETH G. GRAHAM
Stage Manager . .	DAVID LIVINGSTONE

The cast of *You Too Can Have a Body*, performing in the church hall in 1962. They are Brian Baxter, Joan Kennedy, Anne Erskine, John Kelsall, Edward Stewart, Jack Weddell, May Anderson, Alex Linn, Janet Williamson, Pamela Miller, Bill Paterson, Charlie Reid, Joan Bell and Catherine Robertson.

Another group still existing, albeit with a recent new name, was the Womens' Guild. In the 1950s and 60s it had a very dedicated choir which successfully competed in many events. Here they are with one of their trophies, c. 1960.

Hatches, matches and dispatches are major events in everyones' lives. Here is a group of farmworkers from Almondhill dressed in their finery for a wedding in 1950.

Six

Events

As with many communities local events revolve around the village institutions such as the church, the school, the bowling club, etc. Some events are much loved and still continue, such as the annual Childrens' Gala, and some are just fond memories, such as the annual Sunday school trip when the school was closed for the day and most of the villagers piled onto a specially chartered train for the run across the Forth Bridge to Kinghorn on the Fife coast. The Armistice Day parade, as well as commemorating the fallen in war still provides a little bit of peace as the village is closed to traffic for its duration. The picture above shows an early outing by the Sunday school of the Free Church in the nineteenth century, before they joined the annual trip of the Established Church.

The queue down the approach to the station for the train to Kinghorn on the occasion of the Sunday school trip. Many hundreds went on this outing every year until the line was closed.

The Free Church picnic at the turn of the century. The location is unknown, though someone will no doubt be able to identify it. Note that every person in the photograph is wearing a head covering, the boys caps, the men hats, and the ladies and girls in splendid wide-brimmed millinery, though no doubt without much decoration given the rather austere outlook of the church.

National events were thoroughly celebrated at a local level too. Here is the programme to celebrate the Coronation of Queen Elizabeth in 1953. When an event like this takes place the first thing that happens is the establishment of a committee to organise the activity and this one was no exception - to public approbation they had organised a splendid programme.

QUEEN ELIZABETH CORONATION

JUNE 2nd, 1953

SOUVENIR PROGRAMME

Long Live The Queen

FRIDAY, 29th MAY in KIRKLISTON SCHOOL.

Presentation to school children of gifts from County Council Education Committee by Councillor Jas. Todd, J.P. Also Coronation Medals gifted by Messrs Proven, Newliston Arms Hotel.

MONDAY, 1st JUNE.

Coronation Eve Gala Dance. 9 p.m.—2 a.m. Ticket 2/6. R. Connolly's Band. Buffet.

CORONATION DAY.

Old Age Pensioners' gifts will be distributed in the morning.

Kirkliston Pipe Band will play at 10 a.m. to assemble Children and Adults to Masonic Hall 10.30 a.m. for Presentation of Souvenir Gifts to all Children in Kirkliston District Area.

Short Address will be given by Rev. D. Williamson, M.A.

Messrs Forrest Motors Gift to Oldest and Youngest in Village.

A Competition for Best Decorated Houses will be judged by 12 noon and Prizes (see Bills) will be presented at 2.30 p.m.

Assembly in Hotel Car Park for Fancy Dress Competition at 2 p.m. Prizes for 3 Classes—Children, Adults, Old People—will be given at 2.30 p.m. Thereafter a procession will parade round Village to Sports Field at Almond Hill, kindly granted by Wm. Allison, Esq., J.P.

3 p.m. Novelty Sports Meeting. Races for all.

Tea Meal will be given to Children.

Pipe Band will play during afternoon.

8 p.m. Open Air Dancing in Hotel Car Park and Selections by Kirkliston Pipe Band.

Bonfire and Fireworks Display.

Assemble War Memorial, 9.45 p.m. to proceed to Bonfire to be lit at 10.30 p.m.

Fireworks Display, Community Singing and Dancing.

Evening's Entertainment for Old People will be held on a night during Coronation Week.

The coronation of Queen Elizabeth led to country-wide celebration. As part of Kirkliston's effort a parade was held. Here is one of the floats supplied by the distillery carrying the 'Coronation Pierrettes'.

Prior to the introduction of the National Health Service in 1948, all voluntary hospitals relied on contributions from the public for most of their income. Every year the 'Edinburgh Royal Infirmary Pageant' was held to raise funds. Here is pictured the float entered by the Kirkliston malt extract factory in May 1933.

.. Kirkliston ..

Children's Gala Day

TO BE HELD AT

STATION PARK

(Kindly granted by Kirkliston Athletic Football Club),

ON

Saturday, 6th July, 1935.

Children will assemble in the Public School at mid-day, and will proceed therefrom around the Village, headed by the City of Edinburgh Silver Band.

Programme - Price Threepence

Which is given as a donation to the Gala Day Funds, may bring you good luck.

A GALA NIGHT DANCE

will be held in the Masonic Hall, at 7.30 p.m.

The Edinburgh Embassy Dance Band will be in attendance.

The annual Childrens' Gala is now one of the best loved events in the village, being preceded by Civic Week which has a programme of sports, entertainment, fancy dress competition, treasure hunt and pet shows. The Gala Parade is followed by a sports competition on the playing field. Many families, weather permitting, now have barbecues in the evening. The event was established in 1924, the first queen being introduced in 1928. Since then it has taken place annually except during the Second World War and the period 1958-1963. It was revived in 1964 largely due to the efforts of Donald Whyte. Every year brings renewed appeals for committee members and helpers because although most enjoy the festivities and the fun the children have, few give the commitment in time and effort to make it all happen. Above is the programme for the event in 1935. By 1998 the programme had expanded to sixteen pages with photographs.

The highlight of Gala Day is the crowning ceremony. Special staging was erected at the school and the playground filled with spectators. After the school transferred to the new building at Carmel Road the ceremomy was held in Allison Park. From 1997 it has taken place at the new Leisure Centre at Kirklands Park. The pictures seen on this page are both from 1952. The one on the left has Loanhead House, the home of Dr Bentley and later Dr Stewart, in the background.

Gala Day was, and still is, a great excuse for dressing up, as can be seen from the picture above. The queen for a long time was the dux girl of the school, but in more recent times she has been chosen by ballot. In 1952 the queen was Elizabeth Reeder and she was crowned by Mrs Elizabeth Wilson (daughter of Tam Scott the miller), wife of Dr Wilson, by then the village's GP.

The crowning ceremony is always followed by a procession through the village, ending at the sports venue where a picnic lunch is enjoyed. The best carriage available was always used for the queen; in this case in the 1930s the new-fangled and relatively rare motor car took pride of place and Dr Stewart, always having a Daimler or a Bentley was prevailed upon to supply the transport. Nowadays we have reverted to proper horsepower! In the background can be seen the swing park in Station Road, and Bowling Green Terrace adjacent to the bowling green.

An example of modern-day horse power. This is the carriage used for Queen Janice Martin in 1972.

In the week leading up to Gala Day many activities take place - football competitions, treasure hunt and the most entertaining of all, on the Friday evening, a fancy dress competition for both children and adults. It is entered with great gusto and originality by both. Here, left, in 1956, is David Finnie as the legendary Davy Crockett. To be asked to judge the fancy dress competition is to be handed a somewhat poisoned chalice, as the competition is so keen that it is impossible to satisfy everyone. How to win friends and influence people!

David Finnie again, this time as the Ettrick Shepherd in 1957.

Rena Scoular with Ian Mochrie in about
1934 as Darby and Joan.

Again in the 1930s, here is 'Lord Derby' with his horse and jockey in the year that his horse
actually won the race.

Queen Minnie Purves and part of her court in 1933.

Spectators gathered in large numbers to watch the crowning ceremony, though no holidays were given - unlike May 1937 when a three day holiday was granted to the schoolchildren on the occasion of the coronation of King George VI. This large group is enjoying a lovely sunny day in the 1950s.

Above and below are two scenes from the ceremony of 1973, when Carol Havey was crowned by Mrs Margaret McLean. Instead of taking place at the school in Queensferry Road, this event had moved to Allison Park, adjacent to the newly opened school at Carmel Road.

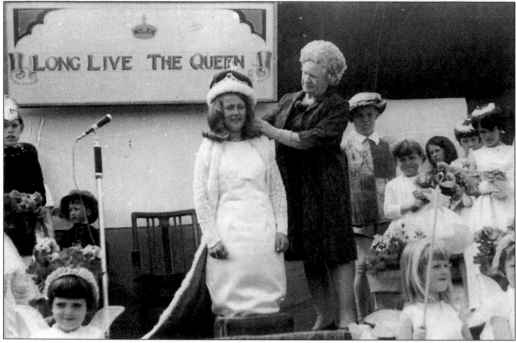

Though most enjoy the occasion it is often a nerve-racking experience for both the queen and the lady who crowns her, as both have to make a speech to the gathered hordes and neither usually has any experience of public speaking. This probably accounts for the somewhat serious expressions on the faces of Queen Louise Wells and Mrs M.J. Dow in 1968.

Every queen has to have her champion and here he is in Main Street in the 1930s. In the background on the left are Arbuckle's Dairy, where the cows, pastured at Foxhall, were milked twice daily, Autumn Cottage and the Masonic Hall. The site of the dairy is now the hotel car park.

There are many other roles enacted by the children. Accompanying the queen (Helen Borthwick) in 1937 are the herald Jack Fairley, train-bearer Rena Scoular and lady-in-waiting Mary Mitchell.

Queen Helen Borthwick and her court in 1937. The herald, Jack Fairley, is clearly 'giving it laldy'!

An early gathering of spectators in 1963. In the background is the schoolhouse used for the crowning ceremony and occupied by the head teacher.

Mrs Hannah Borthwick was for many years the postmistress in the village and was thus known to everyone. She had served the community well and on her retirement in 1956 a collection was made which resulted in the presentation of a clock, seen here being handed to Mrs Borthwick (left) by Dr Isobel Hutchison of Carlowrie. Councillor James Todd presided at the presentation.

The Boys' Brigade had an annual inspection and here is the programme for the one conducted in 1928.

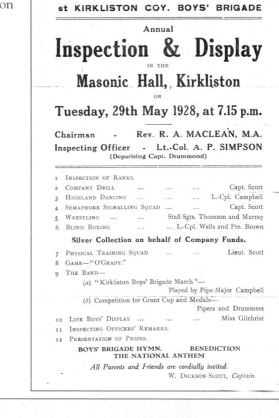

st KIRKLISTON COY. BOYS' BRIGADE

Annual

Inspection & Display

IN THE

Masonic Hall, Kirkliston

ON

Tuesday, 29th May 1928, at 7.15 p.m.

Chairman   -   Rev. R. A. MACLEAN, M.A.
Inspecting Officer   -   Lt.-Col. A. P. SIMPSON
(Deputising Capt. Drummond)

1 INSPECTION OF RANKS.
2 COMPANY DRILL   ...   .   Capt. Scott
3 HIGHLAND DANCING ...   .   L.-Cpl. Campbell
4 SEMAPHORE SIGNALLING SQUAD ...   ...   Capt. Scott
5 WRESTLING   ...   ...   Staff-Sgts. Thomson and Murray
6 BLIND BOXING   ...   ...   L.-Cpl. Wells and Pte. Brown

Silver Collection on behalf of Company Funds.

7 PHYSICAL TRAINING SQUAD   ...   ...   Lieut. Scott
8 GAME—"O'GRADY."
9 THE BAND—
        (a) "Kirkliston Boys' Brigade March"—
                                Played by Pipe-Major Campbell
        (b) Competition for Grant Cup and Medals—
                                Pipers and Drummers
10 LIFE BOYS' DISPLAY   ...   .   Miss Gilchrist
11 INSPECTING OFFICERS' REMARKS.
12 PRESENTATION OF PRIZES.
        BOYS' BRIGADE HYMN.   BENEDICTION
                THE NATIONAL ANTHEM
        All Parents and Friends are cordially invited.
                        W. DICKSON SCOTT, *Captain.*

As part of the celebrations for the end of the First World War, the RAF (then the Royal Flying Corps) contingent from nearby Turnhouse Aerodrome paraded through the village in 1918.

The Scottish Women's Rural Institute has a wide and varied programme during the winter months. One of the highlights, remembered by many, was the Tramps' Ball, held in the Masonic Hall in the early 1970s.

A right bunch of posers! Members of Kirkliston Community Centre Youth Club taking part in the festival Cavalcade of the Edinburgh International Festival on the Lothian Association of Youth Club's float in the 1970s.

Seven
People

Many people have contributed to community life in the village and many are well remembered. Amongst these are members of the medical fraternity, our ministers, shopkeepers, war heroes and generous landowners. This picture shows Dr George Herbert Bentley, surgeon, who occupied Loanhead House, also home to his successor, Dr Peter Stewart. He is shown with his pony and trap, in which he made many of his calls.

Dr Peter Stewart (1882-1945) seated in the back of his well-known car with his chauffeur Tommy Renton in the driver's seat. Dr Stewart was the local GP, and lived in Loanhead House (now the site of Stewart Place, named after him), the stables of which are seen in the background. Loanhead House stood in Queensferry Road.

Purdy Carmichael and his fruit cart in the 1930s. Purdy was a weel-kent face, selling his fruit and vegetables around the area. He kept his horse 'Scrap' in the 'Backlands' between Station Road and the church. His mother sold home-made toffee apples from a table outside her door at 25 Station Road, a very popular call for the local children. Also in the picture are Rita Carmichael, Jenny Arbuckle and George Arbuckle.

'H' Company (Kirkliston) 8th Volunteer Battalion, Royal Scots, before 1914. They held an annual shooting competition for which the Revd Alexander Masson, parish minister 1879-1924, presented a silver rosebowl. The most frequent winners were Sergeant E. Williams and Corporal R. McKenzie.

'Kenspeckle' is an old Scottish word which accurately describes this group of worthies enjoying the sunshine. They are, left to right, Jack Gifford, Jock Forrest, Eckie Wells and Arthur Forbes.

Alex Marandola, of the famous ice cream and chip shop family in a self-portrait taken in a mirror (1959).

Dr Isobel Wylie Hutchison LLD, FRSGS (1889-1982). This remarkable woman lived at Carlowrie Castle. She travelled in Europe and studied languages, although she was better known as a novelist and botanist. She was the first European woman to travel widely in the Arctic regions and wrote extensively about her experiences. She wrote verse, lectured widely, published two plays and contributed to newspapers and journals. The Royal Scottish Geographical Society bestowed on her the Mungo Park Medal in 1934 and in 1949 the University of St Andrews awarded her the honorary degree of Doctor of Laws. A pillar of the community, she served on many local committees and organised and contributed to many charity collections for the disadvantaged throughout the world.

Sergeant Frank Spiers Arbuckle, DCM. He was a serving member of the 8th/10th Gordon Highlanders in 1916 and was awarded the Distinguished Conduct Medal for conspicuous gallantry on the field of battle. The community organised a reception for him at which Dr Stewart gave a speech and Frank was presented with a gold watch and his wife a gold pendant as gifts from the proud and grateful villagers.

The Revd James Law was one of the early ministers of Kirkliston. He served here from 1585 to 1611, a period which saw the union of the crowns of Scotland and England. His first wife was Marion, daughter of James Dundas of Newliston. He went on to become Bishop of Orkney and later Archbishop of Glasgow.

Dr Peter Stewart seen here in his Masonic regalia. He served three years as Right Worshipful Master (1926-28) of Kirkliston Maitland Lodge No. 482. As well as being the local doctor he participated fully in community life, helping to run the reading room, the Kirkliston Nursing Association and was an active member of the bowling club.

In 1906 bands of swarthy aliens were landed by ship at Leith and Grangemouth and headed inland. They were German gypsies from the Baltic who by the immigration laws, were able to enter the country in groups of not more than twenty at a time. The local residents were convinced they were all German spies and the public's fears were fed by the press and by popular literature.

HMS *Kirkliston* was a Coniston Class Minesweeper built in 1954 by Harland and Wolfe of Belfast. She was adopted by Kirkliston and Winchburgh District Council in 1960 and in the period 1960-64 was converted to become the First of Class of the Royal Navy's new minehunters. In 1964 while the ship was at Port Edgar, Lt Commander H.G. de Courcy-Ireland and his fellow officers were entertained in the council chambers in Kirkliston. In 1968 the officers and crew attended a dinner/dance in the Masonic Hall. When the ship returned to Port Edgar after a long tour in the Far East, members of the District Council visited the vessel. She was accepted by the Reserve Fleet at Portsmouth in 1986 and was sent for disposal in 1991. She is seen here passing through Tower Bridge in 1964.

Members of Kirkliston and Winchburgh District Council visiting HMS *Kirkliston* in 1964. With Miss Mary Dunn, Clerk to the Council and District Registrar, are Councillors Walter Proven and Alex Beattie.

From clerk to managing director was the achievement of Duncan McDonald (1881-1968). He was born at Path Brae, the third son of a coal merchant. He went to work as a clerk in Usher & Co. in Edinburgh. He became assistant cashier, then chief bookkeeper and then manager. In 1924 as a result of mergers, he was appointed managing director of the firm of J. & G. Stewart (a subsidiary of the Distillers Co.). He gave much service to organisations in the village.

James Maitland Hog (1799-1858). He was called to the Bar as an advocate in 1822. In 1834 he succeeded to the estates of Newliston in Linlithgowshire and Kellie in Fife on the death of his half-brother Roger. He was an associate and supporter of Dr Thomas Chalmers who led the Disruption in the Established Church. He was largely responsible for the construction of the Free Church in 1843 and was a noted philanthropist of his time, a tradition carried on by succeeding generations of his family. He is buried in the family vault in the parish church.

Mr Charles Gordon, the 'Cruelty Man'. He was employed by the Scottish Society for the Prevention of Cruelty to Animals, and was a popular figure in the village. He lived in the steel house at No. 3 Queensferry Road. He is pictured here about 1950 after retiring.

Miss Helen Maitland Hog, a member of the Hog of Newliston family. She died in 1905 after a life devoted to good works. She founded the Nellfield Home for Cripple Girls and was a frequent visitor to the Free Church-supported Kirkliston Female School, which was sustained in large part by the Hogs.

Three well-known characters pictured in the 1930s behind Rarity's newsagent's shop in the High Street. They are Willie Rarity, S. Gardner and Jim Rarity together with an unnamed ferret.

The Revd James Chalmers Burns was minister of the Free Church in Kirkliston from its establishment in 1843 until 1890. Prior to coming to the village he was engaged at the Scots Church, London Wall, from 1837. He moved into the new Free Church manse in 1851.

Alex Arbuckle was for many years the janitor at the primary school, and then the nursery school and community centre until he retired in 1978. He was and still is a keen gardener, many times winning prizes at the local horticultural show, especially for his sweet peas. He is pictured here in 1975.

Walter Kidd Proven, the last of the Proven family to run the Newliston Arms Hotel, which his family had owned for over a hundred years (see p. 44). He was a member of West Lothian County Council and in common with other businessmen gave generous support to local organisations. He is seen here on Gala Day, c. 1975.

The two 'lollipop ladies' Mrs Catherine Watson and Mrs Elizabeth Glasgow pictured outside the old post office in June 1975. Both were very popular with the schoolchildren.

MY TOWN — N W · E S
YOUR TOWN

KIRKLISTON,
A Walk Down Memory Lane

The cover of a booklet *My Town Your Town*, published by Kirkliston Local History Group in 1994. It was issued in conjunction with a series of conducted walks through the old part of the village and can still be seen in use today as local residents show their visitors around.

Acknowledgments

The Trustees of Kirkliston Local History Archive would like to acknowledge the help, support and materials donated and lent by the community and in particular the following individuals and organisations:

Donald Whyte, Colin and Elizabeth Davies, Stephen and Pauline Crombie, Ina Morris, Marion White, Doreen Gray, Mae Marandola, Sandra McMullan, Gladys Wilson, Scotsman Publications, Express Newspapers, the City of Edinburgh Council, Bruce Simpson, Bill and Nan Blain, Isobel Bowmaker, Kirkliston parish church, James and Marjorie Findlay, George and Helen Reid, Rita McIvor, George Fairley, Jean Lindsay, Anne Thomson, Councillor Eric Drummond JP, Mrs Lesley Bratton, Agnes Cockburn, Anne Lowie, Meg McIntosh, Jim Lawson, A. Kelly, G. Holwill, L. Bowmaker, Betty Hamilton, Janet Wemyss, Ian and Hettie Mochrie.

Donald Whyte, in particular, merits special mention; as well as providing much of the material for this publication, he has an unrivalled knowledge of the history of the area, as exemplified by the four editions of the parish history already published by him.

If we have inadvertently breached anyone's copyright we apologise, and we are sorry if we have missed anyone from the acknowledgments

The Archive as well as providing a rich resource is always on the lookout for new material and if any readers wish to help us by adding to it they can write to us at 19 Station Road, Kirkliston, EH29 9BB.